LOVE IS A TRAVELLER AND WE ARE ITS PATH

LOVE IS A TRAVELLER

AND WE ARE ITS PATH

Poems

MEDINA TENOUR WHITEMAN

THE ECSTATIC EXCHANGE

2016

PHILADELPHIA

FIRST EDITION
ISBN: 978-0-578-17556-0 (paper)
Published by *The Ecstatic Exchange*,
6470 Morris Park Road, Philadelphia, PA 19151-2403

For quotes any longer than those for critical articles and reviews,
contact:

The Ecstatic Exchange,
6470 Morris Park Road, Philadelphia, PA 19151-2403
email: abdalhayy@ecstaticxchange.com
website: www.ecstaticxchange.com

The Ecstatic Exchange was founded by poet / publisher Daniel Abdal-Hayy Moore
in 2005 to publish his life's work of poetry. In addition, two other poets have
been published in the Ecstatic Exchange series: Tiel Aisha Ansari with *Knocking
from Within*, and the present book by Medina Tenour Whiteman. For further
information please visit www.ecstaticxchange.com.

Cover art © Lateefa Spiker 2016
Epigraph calligraphy © Asghar Alkaei Behjat 2016

بسم الله الرحمن الرحيم

CONTENTS

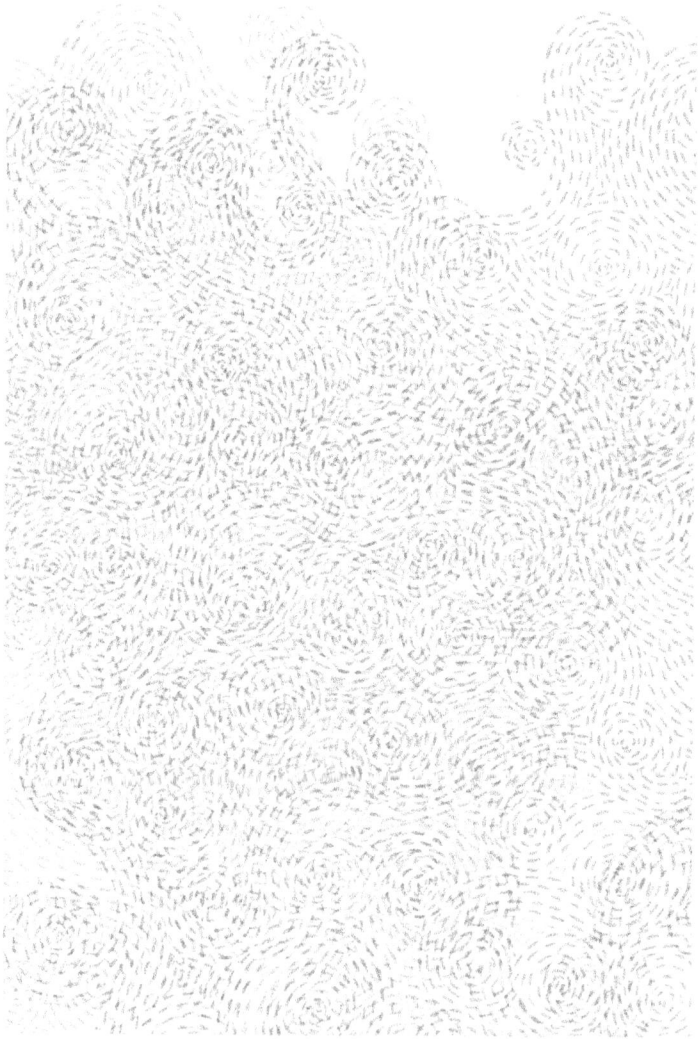

INTRODUCTION

IT'S A GREAT pleasure to introduce to the poetry-imbibing world the first collection of English/American poet, Medina Whiteman, who, as she lives in a mountain town in Spain with her calligrapher husband, raising her three children, and a Sufi Muslim, might be called an "expat" Spanish poet as well. But with her life of travel and study, as well as her skill and maturity, she is also a world poet. You can safely and delightedly come to these poems for spiritual refreshment, she having situated her vivid and exact memory behind our own eyes, so that we recognize our own experiences in her sometimes deceptively breezy accounts. She's a poet who, when she puts her mind to it, and in the grip of an inspiration, *thinks* in poetry. She'll no doubt write her deathbed poem on her deathbed—after all, only three hours after writing *Ten Days Late*, she gave birth, just shy of writing a poem *during*, and in *A Holy Secret Shared*, barely escaped with her life, writing a terrific poem soon after. There's also an echoing "Audenesque" tone here, in her ease of diction, precision of observation, and surprise epiphanies. In its pitch-perfect conversational tone lies a healing, illumined by her love of Allah and His Prophet, peace be upon him, and based in the daily and keenly observed—and it shines. But she gives it all a light touch by not taking *herself* too seriously, while her heart inventories more touchy and touching subjects, motherhood, womanhood, prayer and hypocrisy, in a fine cardiac tuning of mind and eye—poetry's true dimension.

Here are poems that include her wishing to go against type, and her whiteness even, with her name itself proclaiming its bogus prerogative, now wishing she were black, as she says, to blend in with the earth's majority rainbow of dark skin tones:

> I even went to Kenya,
> Tanzania, Zanzibar
> learned Kiswahili well enough
> to fool a local if he did not see my face
> but still one night aboard a boat
> an old man greeted me with
> *"Shikamoo"*: I touch your feet.

Or a visionary take on the soul's calligraphy:

> I've seen the script of an unseen soul
> deciphered letters as they danced Qur'an
> through ink black ocean storms and
> pulled scything oars of *ras* and *zas* to veil
> the bone-white nakedness of paper and
> breathe its dead wood to life.

Or an almost epic high-velocity spirit of enlightened near-mythic woman, in *The Whirler*:

> We sit on the hem of her skirt
> as it rises and falls
> and watch as the cycles
> of heartbreak and hope follow on
> while the whole crazy circus
> spins on these sure feet
> that
> never
> once
> lose
> their
> rhythm

Medina is also a remarkable prose writer, and it seems in her young life she's already been all over the world, and rarely the "beaten path". So many of her poems have a short-story-like feel, such as in *The Loneliest Tearoom in India*, that inserts us into the experience, as she does so well and so often with her sharp photographic precision.

> We left at nightfall
> Delhi still ringing in my ears
> the menacing rickshaw driver
> the protective *tuktuk* driver
> and now this bus, a pencil case
> on wheels conducted by a man with
> lips stained red with betel nut.

Then there's the traumatic finale with a divine twist in the penultimate poem, *A Holy Secret Shared*, that brings together Medina's bright reportage, her themes of motherhood, creative protector and nurturer, and wrings out of real experience a poem of profound resonance whose ending, with its subtle evocation of the Majesty of God, leaves us breathless.

With Medina Whiteman's lively, metamorphosing voice, we have here finely detailed poetic stances on whatever attracts her and her pen, and her heart is here, and its centripetal ripples edge out to our own world and wash over it as if with our own sensibilities—and it is a welcoming thing, a sweet and healing thing to know these enlightened trails.

DANIEL ABDAL-HAYY MOORE

You think you are nothing but a speck,
yet the vast cosmos is unfurled in you!

O mankind, you are a clear book,
by whose letters the invisible becomes visible.

ATTRIBUTED TO SAYYEDINA 'ALI IBN ABI TALIB,
MAY ALLAH BLESS HIS COUNTENANCE

I WISHED THAT I WERE BLACK

I wished that I were black.
So did my dad, it's
a family thing,
like the surname that he gave me:
Whiteman.

But when I got my name
Madinat an-Nur
the City of Divine Light
they didn't get it from a book
for folks whose babies were white.

It came to me from
a Tuareg woman, dark
as coffee beans whose
husband's face was dyed blue
by his turban veil.

Without the searing desert sun
I am a different city
of fluorescent bulbs that
cast cheeks blue
of cloudy English summers that
turn eyelids grey
of library lamps.

In winter I could swear
I were a slow-worm,
a blade of grass growing beneath a tent,
an axolotl.

It really isn't *practical* to be this pale,
having to run for cover and
smother ourselves in zinc-white cream
peeling off the damaged shreds at night
crying on beds that cannot offer comfort.

The message that we seem to get is:
"Don't go outside!"
But I grow wrong when I'm
obliged to hide
a ghosting of the rainbow mind
to match this ghostly shroud.

I wished that I could shed this skin
leave it behind me in a crumpled tube
like a nylon stocking
—oh, the orange tinge
that passes for flesh-toned!

I wished that when I saw my limbs
upon the sheet they'd stand out
in bold relief, real silhouettes,
loud letters on a page instead of these
simpering cut-outs.

I even went to Kenya,
Tanzania, Zanzibar
learned Kiswahili well enough
to fool a local if he did not see my face
but still one night aboard a boat
an old man greeted me with
"*Shikamoo*": I touch your feet.

And when I stayed among
a family from Gujarat and their
five-year-old daughter dusted talcum
powder on her arms—
"So I can look like you!"
I was too mute
with shame
to tell her—
"Don't want to look like *me!*"

But then
I'd wished that I was black.
Or brown, or anything but this insipid hue
that didn't seem to do a thing
to earn its kudos.

What benefit
is it
to break out in a rash when
temperatures rise over twelve degrees?

What savage logic tried to make up
for the gleam, the warmth
the definition that we lacked by making white
the gold standard of all colours?

I still remember
one transcendent moment when
my arm lay next to hers and
my eye falling unthinkingly upon them
registered no difference.

I can't wish that I were black.
These are the clothes that I've been given
a set of overalls to work in
'til they wear out
and the colours split apart
by life's prismatic edge
return
again
to light.

FIRSTBORN

Inched off the mud-soaked cords
you fell asleep in hours ago
food-drunk at the end of the Eid party
face crusted with lamb biriani and
illicit jammy cakes
alien earth now smudging my
pink striped sheets

—MORE WASHING—

You stir and whimper
clutch my face to your sticky
one-year-old cheek
willing my weight to
drag you under again
but sleep is reluctant
a closed-eyed smile
contorts the fat cheek
squashed by my encroaching kiss

You laugh in an ecstasy of touch
my every atom laughs in synchrony
a joy that would keep millions of
crackheads high for over a year
if only they could damn well
synthesise it

—HAH—

it's all for me
me and the jam on the pillowcase

MIRRORS HAVE MOVED UP IN THE WORLD

Once
I don't know when
mirrors were
still pools of water
and the faces in them
downcast, eyes glowing
bathed in reflected light.

When we first learned how we looked
it was as thinkers, mourners,
cradlers of sleepy children.
In this humble curve
we discovered our surprised selves
in unexpected ponds
saw there our souls undressed.

Now mirrors have moved up in the world:
we peer in, eye to eye, shoulders back, jaws set
a photo booth's rectangular frame
we preen our feathers and imagine
how the world must meet us

This reflection's hard as diamond
no curious fingertip
can turn the surface to circles
or drop in a shell to listen for its depth.
The image returns impassively and we
can't wash our hands in it
or take a piece in palm
to scrutinise and scatter.

Some empowerment programme's elevated
mirrors to Wall Status.
Now they're immune to dirty feet
to fishing nets and worn-out rags.
Whatever tears or snarls they witness
there is no change in temperature.
Folds of shawls no longer hang towards
reaching as though in yearning
but drop down shamefully.

If we bow our heads we lose sight
of this vision. In silver
mirrors have at last become
our equals.

BACK WHERE THE PATH BEGINS

Some men love the idea of Islam
for its manliness and its femininity
the gendered garb
strokable beards
scarves like petals round a woman's face
feet marching with a purpose
heart stirred with beauty
but then
the allure of being manlier
kicks a kink in their path
and the lamp shining
on a womanhood bashfully admired
disappears behind a brick wall.
The frowns deepen
the march becomes military
the segregation obligatory
no touching hands—don't break
my *wudu'*—and the beards are now
not thoughtfully stroked but
firmly put in their place.

Chivalry is confused with chauvinism,
gallantry with greed.
Man ascends to the position
he feels is owed to him,
a towering throne from which to judge
how well the womenfolk
are keeping their earlobes covered

lest the animal within him wakes
and he grows so comfortable there
it seems this seat of power was
made purposely for him.

Barbed wire goes up to warn off girls
who might think they
could grow learned and give advice
and every passing decade sees
fewer of them sneaking through the palisade
until the lookouts start confirming
the old ones' belief:
they just don't do intelligence like us.

Meanwhile sunlight dashes
fleet-foot over beardless faces
laughing in private, weeping in private
knowing in private, loving in private
cracking almonds, brewing tea
holding a lost one in their arms
stroking her hair while she finds herself
seeking in dreams and the unseen
for guides whose hands
they are forbidden from kissing
and all this round the crook in the path
where the lamp still flickers
and the watchtower sentries
have forgotten the path begins.

WATCH THE DANCER

She translates longing into leafstorms,
this dancer. She turns the bright beak
of a wheeling lark into a
swooping hand
calls on the lichen's listening creep
the copper seams of dried riverbeds
and races them into our short-lived gaze
so when we watch this dancer sweep and stamp
we don't just see tendons and skin but
algorithms of root and wind
the shooting out of limbs that fruit
sped up halfway to a fly's life span.

When we watch this dancer we
might catch the glacier as it glides
the underwater mass collides
the mountain creeps over horizons
redwoods burst with rings and ride
breakers too vast to fit inside
a human tide. That dancer, she gives
voiceless forces words
their wordless minds still understand
so watch the dancer
if you can.

SWIMMING

No wonder everybody else
has trouble understanding us
our supra-cultural language, our
unapologetic style.

You need eyes
embedded in your heart,
a heart inside your head
to wade through endless
English butcherings of
elegant Arabic verse
—Shakespeare strangled
into semaphore—
gymnastic vision to
skip nimbly over words
pre-branded in the childhood heat of
seen-but-not-heard Sunday schools
to rewrite their burdened meanings.

So pundits write opinions of us
praise and scorn by turns
like experts on the awe of swimming
who, however, never dare to dip their toes
in lake or sea or paddling pool
for fear of getting wet.

ONE DROP

Whenever rocks fall in
resounding in this cavity
a tide rises up unexpected
pouring out in all directions
warm, effacing.

"Allah says with the tongue
of His servant in prayer:
Sami' Allahu man hamidan."
So said the one accustomed to
this waterfall.
It is not us saying it—
not our tongue at all
but His, finding in us
a mirror to gaze into
a pupil to gaze out through
in wonder, legs with which
to wander the jungle
of brick and bamboo
He's brought out of the void
to entertain you with.

When the tide ebbs
this jungle oversteps its boundaries
our new hollowness resounding with
an ache that is forgotten while the play is
projected on its walls;
canned laughter does a good

impression of joy but
nothing else can go this deep
and fill it up to overflowing.

Once you know
the infinity you have within
no flickering lights
can flood you to the brim
like witnessing His Presence
turning the prison of your chest
into the Everything you scrabble for
with hands that could not hold more than
one drop of this fathomless swell.

Go that deep.
Stand the damp and cold
and see how empty all those
entertainments left you
and one sob
one drop that falls
into this void
calls up the breakers
and you'll weep
for all the vacuums
you have ever been
and for how quickly
He rushes in
to fill them.

THE COOLNESS

I used to think I could
excel at being uncool.
You know: eschew
designer logos and
consumerist hysteria
wear charity shop
cast-offs, read
anything but the
Booker shortlist,
blithely laugh at how
few major films
I've watched.

"Oh aren't I clever!"
I would wink into my
mirrored face
with that unstyled crop
of hair—"gamine"—
and ripped-up
souvenir T-shirts.
"Hah!" I'd smirk—
"I've outwitted
the Coolness!"

Sadly, however,
Coolness had merely
infected me in a subtle form
a homeopathic dosage of
Superiority over Crap.

Ramadan is uncool.
No matter what way
you try to paint it,
there is no slogan
or nifty graphic
that can make it hip
to go hungry and thirsty
for fifteen hours straight.
Not to get thin, or reduce
your risk of heart disease
or to get into the
Guinness Book of Records,
but "for Allah".

Fasting, you feel Coolness
being purged out through your pores,
toxic People Pleasing sweated out
and Failure Phobia eliminated
from your flesh as your body
whiles away the foodless hours
burning up your haunches' stores.

The history of you aching to be liked,
to fit in, be admired, or just
not picked on, sneered at, blanked,
forgotten—all that surfaces now,
your brain chowing through old
thoughts and replacing them with
something truly cooling. In this
lucid state you see yourself as though
you've stolen your own diary

and are reading it aloud to screams of
laughter on the back seat of the school bus.

The shrieks die away in time. Hang
in there; you will cringe at first,
but soon you'll feel Coolness ebb to a
distant hum, like a fridge at night, and you
can choose to open it at will, be glared at by
its discriminating light, take out the
carton of juice you needed
and close the door again,
thirst quenched.

BILLOWING

With my son cradled
    in sleep's arm-boat
I switch my thoughts
    from idle chatter to
Surat al-Ikhlas and feel my
    being billow out
in gold embroidered
    velvet.

We glide; a swell of
    wonderment picks up,
impels our craft into the
    surf and through,
aimed for our vanishing
    point.

That is a moment's
    glimpse of one
momentous being who
    never ceased to
surge into the Now,
    setting a course by
stars embedded in his fabric.

This was a being who,
    so inspired with all the
heavens' breaths that there was
    no room left in him for
anything earth-heavy.

On land, his wife had said he was
        the Recitation walking;
out here, though, where
        earth melts to water and
clouds sponge the
        stars' geometry to grey
there is no doubt
        —the words he channelled
tidal in my chest—
        that he, God's peace and
blessings be with him,
        is sailing.

DEAR BIGOT

Dear bigot
—*sigh*—
when you appear on TV
or write your editorials
or seize a woman's *hijab* and deafen her
with a tirade on her lack of British values
—*how very British of you!*—
dear bigot, don't you see?
The more strenuous your conviction
of Islam's threat to humanity
the more your knowledge is shown to be phony,
your intellect imprisoned.
We can see it flailing about in there
behind your stiff, dyspeptic exterior
that flushes green at overt expressions of
Muslimness.

How many times a week do you have
falafels and *batata harra*
at the home of your Muslim neighbour?
When was the last time you popped into
Abdul's Islamic Supplies
— undaunted by the white manniquins
in their sequin-encrusted *abayas*—
and stayed for a *chai* and a chat?

When you complain that Muslims aren't
outraged enough about ISIS,

count how many Muslims
you have befriended who might
litter your newsfeed with their grief.

We're not just good for driving your buses,
for filling your cavities
and selling you cigarettes.
There's a whole world
behind the undifferentiated
Islamic-hued masses
and for all you crow about
how deeply you've studied the subject
read those editorials
watched those war zone clips
tell me if you've ever asked
a flesh-and-blood Muslim what they think,
how they live, who they are?

Without those voices
your condemnations are
a drone strike on an unseen village
by a 19-year-old video game junkie
with a lethal excess of patriotism.
What does your myopia make you?
An ostrich, or a mole?
Look how your heart has been papier-mâchéd
with pages of The Telegraph!

Break out, dear bigot!
You aren't so monstrous under all that crust,
nor are we. See us:
we are human.

Allow room for our failings
and we can forgive your blindness, too.
We are only trying
always trying—
still trying.

A WOMAN IS A JUMBLE SALE

A woman is a jumble sale
a riot of obsolete cassettes
that hold nostalgic value
holey socks and too-small
suede jackets that would look good
if only...if her body were...
(still, the thought of looking hot in it
was worth every penny.)

And you, male browser,
scanning through her
chipped gravy boats
scuffed pumps
retro plastic sunglasses
that still make her grin to wear them
you, oh male peruser,
have the choice whether to scorn
her history of bad taste and saunter
off in search of more impressive tat
or
to riffle patiently through her EPs
and cheesy paperbacks
(remembering that this is just the junk
she's willing to show the public)
and chance upon that rare 1880s
engraved silver compass
she was always looking for
someone to give to
and the glow in your eyes

appreciating it
turns all the trinkets into treasure
at the feet of a queen.

Don't you see, oh male desirer?
It is your admiration
that draws out her beauty.
She sees your delight
and opens the box
hidden under the foldout table
full of more wondrous things
the ones she didn't want to muddle up
with the broken fake Rolexes.

Don't you see, oh male
seeker of the sublime?
She embodies it
when she feels your awed gaze
lighting her up in a corona.
Just as He said,
"*I am in the opinion of My servant*",
want only this Beauty
and she will dazzle you with it.
Love her
and she will give you
reason to.

THE BLOODLESS BUTTON

Syria is being bled white.
The metaphor is painful—
death paints all our inner
skins the same shade:
pomegranate juice.

Tall strangers in navy suits
make bleak press conference
speeches saying We Can Help—
but look: this aid comes by way
of dropping bombs from
bloodless planes, no ruby drink
to risk, deaf to the howls,
dumb to reply to the question
How did you think this would help?

And the whiteness that somehow survives
standing, walking in its nice navy suit
is watered by some other fluid
replaced the day he swore to represent
his voters—not as fellow humans, but as
holders of the pens that ticked the box
beside his name. And then
he'll call on human values, courage,
heroism, compassion, moral codes
while his own moral code is lying
in a pool in Tahiti, sipping champagne.

This bloodless lust for throwing in
another murderous device and calling it
compassion, better than standing back
and doing nothing, is the creaking of
machines in need of oil; there's no soul
in there to suffer for their lie, only
the shine of brass buttons on navy suits
a team of hairdressers and make-up dusters
to ensure the machine passes for human.

Give me a man in tatters
alive and hurting
let me hear the things he says
unshepherded by press release
and ceramic teeth; let me
perceive the rotten pieces, scuffed shoes,
zits and burnt-out coat—
I want to see he knows the end result
from bitter first-hand sight
before he tries to make me see
the need to push
that bloodless button.

VAST FORESTS
(Poem written while fasting)

Everything's a reminder of absence
the metallic mouthfeel
gurgling plumbing
phone call from my beloved in
another time zone
breath from mouths too dry to talk sense
the dinner we started preparing too early

There is longing even in lost *miswaks*
displacement in a pair of shoes
clothes that came on boats from China
rugs bought in Turkish bazaars
sold by city folk but woven by peasant women
in alternate landscapes
pineapples pressed in Costa Rica
to be consumed in London, E9

Everything is gone before it is touched
en route to somewhere else
nothing homely, nothing whole
nothing original, nothing owned
these things are not ours, never were
our hands have never touched anything
only seen sense-pictures made inside

We are sealed
hermits against an outside unreal

always being taken somewhere else
and sold
and altered
and blown into a different mould
so nothing is new or alive
only
whatever we live first-hand
within the vast forests within
that no-one else can take
that no-one else can taste unless
they leave their heavy cloaks and fly
into those forests with you
or you do likewise and
drop your body-dunes
to roam across their plains

BEFORE SHE OUTGROWS YOUR ARMS

Birth takes you deep
beneath humus into
an earth alive and
elemental

The quiet of a forest
patient burden of an ant
an acorn growing
anonymously underground

Amazons with gritted teeth
a lioness predating
crash of
whale's tail on sea
fearsome swell of
tsunami

Then
tenderness in torrents
bliss of being more than one
cheeks glistening with thanks
for briefly being someone's world
before she outgrows your arms
drifts off across the waters
and forms her own island:
for now she is
a peninsula of you

FOR SENSE OR SILENCE

If the *Ummah* is one body
then we are all brittle bones
skin grown armoured
out of fear of
speared looks

Meanwhile collapsing organs
leave lacunae in their wake
hollows that cringe and cramp
and invite hauntings

Our veins have dried to desert rivers
joints creak arthritically
only so far, shaking at the idea
of stretching any more

Between the mummified exterior
and the limping core
there is an emptiness
that reaches out for union
sighs for solidity
whistles like hilltop pines
for sense or silence

My voice sings into this void
this concert hall denied of concerts
stifled by a plaster casing
that was created to protect

but the wounds need air;
our bandages are soaked through now—
to keep them on we risk
a gangrene on our souls

Listen quietly as you unwind them:
there is music in the rattling of our bones
in the weeping of our tissues
in the way we scrape our heels
along the ground

It joins the leaves' percussion in the wind
the insects' string section out on the lawn
the whisper of oranges as they fill with juice
the sparrows chittering in code and the
deep heaving of planets
drawing harmonies out of space—
that is a song to get us up and dancing again!

Quivering brings vibrato
to our parched throats—trembling
makes the timbre believable
and the tunes that rise
unwritten in that loss
score our hymn

AN ENEMY LIKE LOVE

Every lover knows
to be immersed
there must be
complete destruction:
broken windows, torched cars
private armageddons
that tear off the scales
to leave the naked skin beneath
convulsing with surrender,
a happy death, a surging through,
a racing out.

The cup that
used to overflow is lying
in smithereens on the floor;
its contents heated to a mist
invading parched throats,
parting lips and waves.

With every kick, each
poison dart another
vanity balloon is burst,
another reason for misgivings
struck down; whole
battalions of armoured
riot police are scattered,
plastic shields futile against
an enemy like love.

With all this revolution
my heart's tin is beaten to
a lamp's gold curve, now just
waiting for your listening touch
to light it.

TWO STATES

Two states compete
for my longing:
one, a room for living in with wood fire
burning behind smudged glass
a heap of books, some open
wet socks hung on the back of a chair
a bowl of fruit, some cut and not yet brown
shoes toed off and left at irreverent angles
something humming in a corner,
processing dried fruit or data and
even when the room is empty of people
it is thrumming with the echo of them.

The other is wall to wall cabinets
neatly closed, dust-free,
windows freshly Windexed
a bank of new steel iMacs
working glitchlessly
leather seats arranged to look casual
but there are no crescents of coffee
on the coffee table or
crumbs on the geometric rug
no piles of dry clothes to fold
or smeary glasses waiting
to be washed.
A fug of central heating
closes throats to a polite silence. *No ash!*
Double glazing drowns out

the noise of the neighbour's dog;
here one can concentrate
there are no cobwebs to sigh over
or interruptions by small children
thumping each other over felt tip pens.

Behind the cabinet doors are
stationery supplies to last
'til kingdom come
fresh orders of necessities
have been made weeks in advance
for there is no chaos here to hinder
business, no boring list of frets
to get on top of before projects
can fructify. This orchard
yields polished apples
red and round
without pockmark or warp
grown under supervision
under daylight lamps
to industry standards.

The latter is where a half a million
is small change, where minds
boil and brew great schemes
reach nebular heights
dynamic people drop in
to ping ideas about and
everything occurs on time.

The former, though, is the only place
my mind will sink its toes

into soft soil, send down
taproots that drink from hidden aquifers
and while my hands are pairing socks
cutting paper snowflakes
making tea stains on the table
the real business is happening
on another schedule, one that
sees a calendar like any other piece of earth-to-be
and makes misshapen fruits
that fall and lie embedded in nettles
as edible ore in the ground of home.

The only guarantee
this place gives me is that
nothing will be perfect
(at least I can't be disappointed);
here the products hug me back
leave me love notes in scrambled English
and the day they leave
and my rug goes for weeks without
a hint of a crumb
I might finally get something done
if I can only stop myself
from spending all day blinking
in surprise at the quiet
and missing the mess.

ON THE BOOT OF UKRAINE

The standoff is startling
pale-faced, clean-shaven
as patient as snow
on the boot of Ukraine

Meanwhile, bones grow in babies
floors dirty themselves
muttered grumbles repeat
between broomstick and brain

Men are ranged in steep banks
as though cliffs ploughing on
to raise slow-cresting mountains
on foreign terrain

But at home, plates sit
crusted with rice and cheese
washing needs taking in
safely out of the rain

Whispered terrors of war
thread through emails and towns
ignite testosterone
fan a wildfire chain

But the people still pee
move their bowels most days
dead leaves, soap and hair
still encumber good drains

That momentous decision
of conflict or peace
raises all of our stakes
queries what is humane

Yet food and clean water
still need to be sought
foraged, stolen or bought
hunted, fished, caught or slain

Ambulances are readied
tanks, vast submarines
great causes flush hot
in the president's veins

While his mistress is ironing
silk slips that he gave,
asks the housewife next-door
what works best on wine stains

Rallied shouts float above roof-
tops: "Fight for your rights!"
though the war's still a theory,
immanent the campaign

Housewives beat out their rugs
water aubergine plants
beetles creep inside bottles
and goats block the lane

The diplomats clinch it:
troops retire, blank and
brotherless, silent
to soften pride's pain

Cotton sheets heave and snap
cats thieve mackerel heads
hair is wincingly brushed
bowls of oranges arranged

lovers long for reunion
and while planets drift
deaf to all mankind's bluffs
someone calls out God's names

but down here on earth
the soil's still brown as boots
ever pounded beneath
the boot of Ukraine

THE EYE THAT BLINKS

I've seen the script of an unseen soul
deciphered letters as they danced Qur'an
through ink black ocean storms and
pulled scything oars of *ras* and *zas* to veil
the bone-white nakedness of paper and
breathe its dead wood to life

I watched as pirates scuttled in with
knives between bared teeth boarding
the calligalleon to plunder its gold
only to find the hull bare
as a ribcage in a grave
and so they slunk off to murder
the minutes elsewhere

I saw a secret paradise erupt
beneath their metal-blinded eyes
spill out an ecstasy of life
in frothing origami waves
while pilot birds guided the ship
to shore in graceful *fathas;* this
was not an idle scrawl by absent hand
but an island alive with the artist's
deepest heart-form crashing
freedom-bound through paper surf
to meet the eye that drinks it in

the eye that blinks with thirst

A CASCADE OF SHATTERING GLASS

Under a cascade of shattering glass
waves glide beamingly overhead
opening light through their million edges
in ways that make sunshine new
(I am not used to this parasol)
and the premonition of pain is
blurred by the beauty.

Next minute
we're walking chest-deep in fracture
the heat rushes up to heal hairline cuts
that fray hearts to a halo
but legs that appear to be shredded keep walking
mind takes note of extraneous things
—the cats have ran out of biscuits;
breakfast'll have to be leftover rice—
yet mid-morning the thought of her friends and twin sister
washing her, as though asleep in their arms,
perfuming the long hair that once hung in a braid
from a white Astrakhan hat, dressing her
still-warm limbs,
and the silence of her song forever stilled
return and ache into my corners.

Now again the brilliance rises:
the way she could call up a wave of harmonies
from a fidgeting room
turn strangers into heart-mates
and awe at her fearless direction,

blunt honesty when something sounded wrong,
set a lamp beneath this ceiling of glass
and make the inside more dazzling than all
the stars crowding down at us
peering in through the clear roof of this moment
wishing they too could know grief.

THE WHIRLER

At dawn
if you creep up quite close to my brain
you will hear all sorts of snorts and grumblings
as a motley crew of workers creak out of bed
getting the show ready for the world
if it wants it.

Birdbeak is clearing her throat
in anticipation of the
Debating Society's daily throng of one
(herself) to be quietly seated
for her assassination of opinions
to begin.

"Sirs," she squawks, "and
Madams, I put it to you
that the hippie ideal is a
shallow pretense of
great wisdom,
dressed up in some tatty
Guatemalan threads
smelling of Nag Champa
and sweat. They
disdain the alternatives
to their Alternative,
calling their dogma
Chilling The Hell Out
and Letting Things Flow,

whilst fuming inside
is a small moustachioed
fascist dictating how everyone
should live. I think
I have stated my case
rather well, don't you?"

Meanwhile, in a room
littered with broken guitar strings
and passed-out partygoers
a *cantaora* is rising at this
most unholy hour to catch the
bombona man (the gas
bottle's low). Her wild
red-streaked hair is still
nest-like, mascara from
last night's performance
a mad hash of black
under mad flashing eyes.

She doesn't deign to talk;
her voice rips the air
after midnight, when lava
built up in her chest
will scorch ears in a cascade of
hoarse-throated passion,
heels stamping, hips snapping,
hands grabbing invisible oranges
plucking them free from trees
searching for real sweetness
amid anguish. Her singing

is melody inverted, no
little girl laughter tinkling in
its moan. She is pure, raw, hot
woman-fire, calling for rain
and her song spits and crackles
with sobs of ancient pain but
this morning she's grumbly
a dressing-gowned mess
in pink fluffy slippers, fresh
cigarette on her lip, scowl
sending Señor Bombona scurrying
away to another address.

Outside in the garden
beyond La Lava's room
in the tangle of green which the
lawnmower won't reach
Earth Child's
butt is straight up in the air
(the blood rushes down to
the head, very good for the
pituitary gland, so they say).
Her hair straggles about
ants crawl round her ankles
dirt underlines darting fingers
that fondle the weeds:
some of them she nibbles,
recalls their Latin names
and nutritional benefits
oxygen-drunk in the company
of leaves.

Up in the attic
a songwriter huddles,
chewed Biro and paper
cradled in hands that
close and open, sculpting
the shape of this feeling
or that. Now music is
called out of emptiness,
notes throb and clash and
reverberate in the wooden vessel
pressed against her chest.
A creature's being birthed
through the soundhole
intuitive action
essential to let it emerge
head first, twisting when
twisting's needed to free
its four limbs: no rush.

It's born and she licks it
into life, cleans away
the viscera that kept it
waiting in sacred darkness
safeguarding its secret
'til it tastes air and is kissed
by the angel that makes it
forget all it knows. The song
is alive and the silence that
grew it is gone.

In a space
at once inside and out
there is a fifth being,
her head tilted lightly
eyes closed to soak up the
Grace as it falls soft as
petals, melting into her spin
as she whirls in her own
private snowstorm. Her
white robe unfurls in a
circular sail billowing
out in an oceanic wave
transcribing airborne
acrobatics on unseen
vertices of *Dunya* and
Here-and-Now Paradise.
One arm is raised up
to let Light trickle down,
cross her shoulders and wet
the bare earth, cool the
faces of all the other inmates
in a rose-water mist.
But the Whirler herself is
immune to sensations,
so rapt in the Real that
no substitute tries to convince her.

The Whirler is mostly ignored
(though the sight of her levitating
UFO-like over towns and
green mountains should

make us break out into
a cheer). But she's so
bloody real that the
rest of this outfit
gets bored with her
serenity.

We sit on the hem of her skirt
as it rises and falls
and watch as the cycles
of heartbreak and hope follow on
while the whole crazy circus
spins on these sure feet
that
never
once
lose
their
rhythm.

THE LONELIEST TEAROOM IN INDIA

We left at nightfall
Delhi still ringing in my ears
—the menacing rickshaw driver
the protective *tuktuk* driver—
and now this bus, a pencil case
on wheels conducted by a man with
lips stained red by betel nut.
I sat at the front. I wore a loose headscarf
but how to mask the whiteness?
The woman beside me gladly made
sign language conversation for a while
'til our vocabulary ran out.
All this time a man with a white
handlebar moustache was scrutinising me.
"Madam," he said at last, "when you are asleep
you look like doll."
I could not sleep much after that.

The turns, so thoughtfully marked
with yellow signs that wrung their hands
in big black letters:
"Always Alert Aviod Accident"
"Someone At Home Wants You To Return Safe"
while the betel in the driver's blood
pressed the pedal into the floor
almost wearing a hole
turning the wheel with violent grace
and even though rocks tumbled down
into the glossy void over the edge

down in the Himalayan crooks
we could not see them land.

The wheels kept their footing.
My stomach, however, did not.
It slid about upon the vinyl seats
barely contained by my thin skin
wringing itself to squeeze out
that cheap *thali* I had wolfed
but when we stopped, blinking by moonlight,
the latrines seemed worse so
on we oscillated
round the mountain's shoulders
road a snakeskin through the glacial dark
and at one moment someone asked me
"What's your name, Madam?"
I answered honestly. They wondered
why? So I replied. They shrieked
with glee, or horror:
"She's a Muslim?"

In between the wracking pains now
I was sobbing, still too teenaged to
admit the tears to strangers.
Finally two young men with
much more reasonable moustaches
offered me some herbs for stomach pains
and then a *bidi*, which I smoked out of
the back window. The others asked my pardon,
though I was not still sure if this were
initiation into some strange
Indian social rite.

As dawn let colour flood back down
the mountains, trees emerged
a perpendicular gorge
a river cavorting at its feet.
We paused for breakfast and latrines.
This time I was not so particular.

The *chai* was good, the teacakes edible.
Steel cups; you must avoid the rims
for hygiene's sake. Low knocked-together
wooden stools and tables. The loneliest tearoom
in India. We embarked again,
our destination Manali, town of hashish,
long-eared rabbits, dreadlocked Germans and
vast heights. But Manali, curious as it was,
never did shake off that bus trip.
Once we reached Leh
after four by four, trek, pony ride
and rooftop hitchhike
I did the journey back
by plane.

ON ONE FEATHER

Books have become my butterflies
alive for just one day or less
before the surf of routine
comes crashing down overhead
raising my feet from ocean bed
helterskeltering me along the pages
soaked and distant.

Books have become a bus stop
scratched with teenage loves
willing the passersby to want to flee
their own lives for an hour
a day, a night journey to foreign towns
a round trip when the back page
flips shut.

Books have become my hoopoes
hooting some way off, a flash of black
and white too fluttersome to stay
when I approach. Gone!
Perhaps I'll catch a feather.

And on one feather I can fly
hit thermals so high just one line
could make me a kite and glide
over terrains no-one will ever see but I.

On just one letter I could ride
to caverns, canyons, cascades

altitude lakes blue as eyes
dry, red-streaked rocks
corporeal dunes
spruce forests so dense
sounds fight to reach our ears
clearings where stand in moonlight
roundhouses of polished wood
in which are found circles of
lovers of the Word.

They must exist!
And I am going
by any vehicle necessary
to find them.

TEN DAYS LATE

Can't heft my waddling self to town
because my abdomen's too round
the exclamation will resound
"She's—got—to—pop!"

The thing no shrill onlooker knows
the way a peaceful labour goes
you melt like snow, tectonic slow
ain't—no—"chop—chop".

External forms are softened, blurred
colours blotch, sounds get misheard
and a string of clever words
stum—bles—head—long;

By now the pressure on the flesh
is causing twinges something spec-
ial and you lumber like a fresh-
ly—beached—du—gong.

Still this baby's so serene
warming his toes against my spleen
upside-down he is, it seems,
le—vi—ta—ting;

And so I'll tell those who opine
that my girth is saturnine
"I'm not post-date – we are just fine
me—di—ta—ting!"

(Three hours after writing this poem I was in labour... and at 9:05am on March 11th 2015, Taj Farid was born)

AFTER BIRTH

The carob seedling that took two years
to grow two feet was planted over
half of the placenta that took
nine months and eleven days to develop
and forty minutes to birth
into a bucket, so dense with my blood
it looked like crushed raspberries.

There are pieces of me buried all over:
one beneath a pomegranate tree
in a nearby Andalusian garden,
another under an apple tree in a
Norfolk farm—the only one in the orchard
to fruit the first year.

The goodness of meat
that once nourished my babies
before they opened their mouths to eat
the meat that died in the act of birth
now feeds those stalks and leaves,
sipped thoughtfully by xylem and phloem
(words I learned eighteen and a half
years ago, the only ones that have
travelled forward from Science GCSE)
and plumps out fruit that I
shrink from eating lest it be
cannibalism:
my flesh into theirs,
vegan victuals from viscera.

Parts of me are already underground.
The backward-rolling echo of tombs
reaches me half-asleep, feeding
a dozing baby, not knowing if an hour or
ten minutes have passed, the way
the mind dashes forward during prayer
and a third *rak'ah* feels like a fourth.

Time is plastic when one has already put
an organ into a tiny grave, when one's footprint there
roots the soul to the soil. It owns me now
in three segments, yearning for the last piece
(currently in my freezer) to join them underneath
an avocado sapling, followed one day
by the rest. Like taproots busy seeking
low lying aquifers there are unseen ligaments
that tie me to the world
so that the hot air balloon of my thoughts
—straining against its ropes—
does not spiral off and be vaporised
by the sharp edge of the atmosphere.

A GAME WAS NOT JUST A GAME

Things used to be so important.
A game was never just a game;
it was
a landmine running dare
across the football pitch
a death-or-ecstasy event
of hula hoops and
fences scaled
apples scrumped
neighbours evaded
mettle put to trial
burned 'til it smelts
and smokes away
the impurity of youth.

We weren't playing;
baffling fragments of the
grown-up universe were being
unencrypted by chalk-fingered
quantum physicists
in alice bands
germinating theories
to explain the adult mystery
in skipping song.

An evening in with
bath bubbles or
learning a new word

drawing horses better
than ever before
while the sunshine
on the rope swing
slid coolly to the grass
meant perfect harmony—
harm within these walls
impossible.

Loyalty did not mean
supermarket cards but
pinpricked fingers
beatings taken out of solidarity
troth pledged until
death or at least next summer
when everything would have changed
and so would we.

A fickle insult would
for one volcanic moment
dismantle all that was
familiar and good
the edifice of our own worth
reduced to wiry rubble
all hope melted
sucked away before we
had the chance
to wallop them back.

Every birthday scratched a tally mark
a tattoo of distinction from

the embarrassment of being small
on pinch-rouged faces
one milestone closer
to the distant, golden land of the
incomprehensibly big
not knowing
when we emerged there
just how dusty and distracted
we would be and longing
for another go
on the rope swing.

SALE ON AT THE DERVISH STORE

It's not hard to look enlightened.
The words, the gaze, the faraway smile
are only a YouTube tutorial away.
It's easy to wrap a scarf round your head
drape robes to the floor and listen
as whispers confirm your piety.

It's such fun to dress up holy. There's
always a sale on at the dervish store
the perfect cap for him, on-trend
scarves for her, tied just right
for your degree of righteousness.
And sighing over lowly work
—duties of motherhood,
bleaching communal kitchens, treating
grandma's bedsores—
all of that comes absolutely free!

It's simplicity itself to bow
and press my brow into the ground
a metronome of shape and sway
but what's hard is the shudder
and the flood that inundates the mat
when it's no longer about being looked at
and the urgency of living truth
surges in like an unexpected guest
and stares me into tears.

It's not enough simply to brush past
all those heathens in the ice-cream aisle, your
turban towering higher than their beehives,
to dedicate your days to praying
while your partner has to pick up all the bills,
to lecture all the world on all their faults
while you gaze at a mirror that is
airbrushed by your very eyes.

But that is not this path. That's just
another fetish of a frock, this time with
a sanctioned length, a humble cut;
it is Milan for monks, catwalks for castaways
too caught up touting their tatters
to notice the bottle that shores up
bringing them hope
or pain
but always
something real.

That is the hardest part
of the hardest path
but the hardest of all
is wanting it.

DEEP FOR PROTECTION

Have I wasted my time?

The mountain aerie
I set my telescope to
still blinks far off
barely ten breaths
closer than a year ago

Meanwhile
I've
     planted holy basil
made ten tinctures
a thousand meals
stuffed toys from scraps
sent a million comments into
the invisible breeze to land
on laps in far-off lands
cleaned endless dirty floors
teeth   dishes   loos
limbs of the immense entity
called Family that never ceases
to be hungry or make mess

I've
     pruned a dozen trees
staked up tomatoes
pulled ticks out of stray dogs
even read a child a story while a tick

was being removed
from between his buttocks

I've
        built stone piles by rivers
tested homemade bows and arrows
started many books and had to
put them down at some small crisis
cut back weeds only to watch them grow
locked gates and opened them
so many times it seems the memory alone
will wear out the metal
made paper darts
cardboard castles complete with
drawbridges and keeps
made friends at playgrounds
sang at one man's funeral
fasted, prayed, forgot
and was reminded

In this vast wheel
that never stops nor moves ahead
what seems to be routine
are centripetal forces throwing me
back to the centre, daring me
not to get dizzy

The aerie's flitting wings
beckon with copper plumes
urge me to go beyond the humdrum
make a life that's bigger. I

hear the call and inner eagles
rustle in their nest; but
they have not yet
yearned enough
not ached sufficiently
to flee the sticks and fluff
and taste high mists
achieve what no bird's ever
dreamed of doing

The wheel spins on
so slow it aches;
success glints brilliant eyes and if I
were not so needed I'd have
stolen its wings by now I'm sure
(see how I make excuses?)

Meanwhile my nest
appears to float above
the whirling motion underneath
we are an island of debris
that currents nudge and kick
so are we lost at sea?
Or is this what must be
so that we do not sink?
Is that blue mountain nothing but
a mirage sent to keep my head from
gravitating centrewards?
Is it a spurious success that winks
disdainfully, shrinking my daily sweat
to a blank space on a resumé?

Lulled by the constant turning
eggs are warmed within
ideas nose the eggshell cracks
that would let lethal icy air inside
if they were up that high;
instead I keep them close
deep for protection
while the tide moves us
imperceptibly on

THE VACUUM

The door swings open
pivots lazily like a child
hanging from a door handle
thinking holiday thoughts

Your breathing shudders
some unknown fear ebbing
to amnesia in your sleep

I must get up, get something done!
I peel you off as slow as branches grow
breaking the vacuum that loving you creates
and lever you back against a cushion where you
splay out, mouth an open dot

A stripe across your cheek
from the seam of my shirt

the outline of your ear
imprinted on my chest

POEM ON LITTLE SLEEP

I walked into town naked
rode the bus naked
gave a public address naked
improperly ended conversations naked
on nightmare mornings caught trains
at chilly stations naked
bought croissants naked
sent emails naked
—*they won't guess*—
enlisted male help
when I locked myself out naked
everyone must be so well-bred
to gaze down instead
pretend a cotton slip
defends the naked backs and legs
I take precautions
wrap round cloth printed with
bold distracting themes
an amulet against the demon gleam
but what shines through is
more touchable than flesh
no cell involved nor nerve
but penetrating to the quick
there comes a sight that sometimes
takes a long-cut through
human perception
just to share the ride
defies the laws of physics

this eye needs no bundle of optic fibres
it's connected in a million strands to
visions scattered wide in unseen lands
and seeing has no nationalistic pride
seeing sees itself
seeing sees through all this
these borders of dirt and cloth
it needs no permission to raise veils
any more than we need to
ask ourselves leave
to undress
any more than a hand would need
to ask permission right before
it grabs yours as the floor gives way
there are no rights to clamour for
when all is almost lost

We protest our innocence naked
with guilt bruising our ribs
extol our brilliance naked
with doubt in weals on arms and hips
proclaim nobility naked
with shame pen-red on fingertips
perhaps our dignity's eclipse
goes unseen to human eyes
but I know there is One Who
sees right through it

LIVING ROOM IN PALESTINE

(Written during the 2014 Israeli assault on Gaza)

I talk with Palestine on Skype
from a dining table in East London
an Arab friend in Israel translates
a tourism brochure while I type
in Arabic so slow my fingers cringe

Her living room is brightly lit
a baby squeals in another room
while we discuss the right word
for *pergolas* and *romantic*, the *agaves*
that Lorca called *"petrified octopi"*
and lanterns in Granada's Moroccan quarter

Our sadness flits behind outbursts
of geraniums on balconies
hides in vaults
of the Alhambra and *hammams*
flavours olives, lemons and almond cakes
things brought to Spain by Muslims
who were then crammed into a province
as populous as the rest of Spain put together
and finally exiled, massacred or muted

Now an airplane flies over her village
a fragment of Palestine in the middle of Israel
my heart stops for a second that lasts years

but she goes on looking up words
the dictionary pages lisp and
the *adhan* goes for *'isha*
loudspeaker overpowering our work
for a minute that I wish would last an eon

We return to Sacromonte and prickly pears
armoured sweetness loaded with seed shrapnel
Palestine as close as news reports and
distant as home

PHYSICAL DHIKR

It passed through in the milk, crossed
placenta's lifeblood bridge
entered muscles, bones, capillaries, a
synaptic code message
heard it sung as I was rocked in
an ocean that does not drown
kept in perfect floating stasis
unbiased by up or down
learned the meaning of protection there
of never feeling fear
an anti-gravity encasement
warmed by nearness of the Near
had it rhythmically taught to me
in mother *hadra* dance
listened quietly as she sang it
in my waking-sleeping trance.
Now whatever questions pose themselves
like mirror-gawking girls
reflecting endlessly upon their looks
their freckles and their curls
there is something in my cells I
can't disdain or regret
there's remembrance in my body—
I can't physically forget.

ONE'S NO LONGER ONE

How warped we have become
that one's no longer one
necks outstretched but bound
constantly gulping air, the knot
in this elastic reach from head to heart
striking the deep yell dumb.

There is an understanding
that is not being understood,
an aged woman in a tree
howling a warning down to us
of mudslides roaring down the hill but we
are more preoccupied with
sawing up her oak for fuel.

"One's no longer one!"
she weeps into the waning green.
"You've longed for so long
to be different,
for each one of you to be a single one,
separate and round,

"But split off from your whole
you have become so very small,
ions spinning unearthed
round your steady Core."

How warped things have become
that one is not enough for merely one,
solitude old hat, simplicity passé;
how hunger loves to make more things to want
but leaves the bill to us.

"One's no longer
one!" we gloat into our calculating claws
that shred togetherness
and while we're scrabbling for scraps
our eyes stay
green as hunters.

THE CHASE

In the women's *dhikr* today
there are birds
circling overhead
darting between us as we sit
huddled in animal skins

Then voices strike up a rhythm
baby heels awake and walk sliding
against my muscle walls

At first the voices take different paths
through the woods but soon find
well-worn tracks
the low ones close to the ground pause
and listen for approaching presences
while high ones soar through scraps of leaves
to get a clearer view

Now the footbeats fall faster as lights
are seen from a clearing ahead
a shaker starts up
shakes out the shopping
the frisson of fear at pennies
small as pebbles in hands
and a lolloping, skipping drum thud
beside me groans as
arms held tight over sharp-cornered duties
lay down their loads on the ground

while the chase picks up speed
new notes drop in as
bright circles of coloured paper fall
lit from above, overlapping

Our *la ilaha ill'Allahs*
swell in waves, move
the water in our cells
sacs of amnia, the bottle
in the centre of the circle

We pull closer

The *hadra* starts slowly
at first mere breaths
Hayy, Hayy, Living, Living
my eyes are shut
my baby's perhaps
open and intrigued
seeing the words
calligraphed in my membranes
and singing too with water
instead of air

Now we stand and sense
the togetherness surge
one baby dozes
another wakes
a *Hayy* runs through our
linked hand circuit
as each woman takes her rhythm

bouncing
swinging
shivering with delight
the ones caught in between
dancing on a squint

The birds are punching holes
in the forest canopy now
we pant our *Hayys* because we run
feet levitating with hunger
coloured circles falling
snow-like on the
threshold of the clearing
of the garden
and the Gardener
is already here

INKWISE WEST

In the small of the night
I left my body on the crumpled sheet
rose up like heat waves from an August street
twitch of fingers only pebbles
settling on the bed of a lake.

I spilled over, up, past historical
borders, the map my body made
on cotton now obsolete.

To be suspended like that for an instant
would have been golden enough but
the present picked up its moorings and ran,
spreading inkwise West, outrunning
the dusk, branching apart as veins in
leaves to meet the air rising in
other chests. It carried me
in its great transcontinental rush,
recognising itself in every face,
the blood of the moment rejoining
that eternal, palpable loop from which we
draw our sleeping breaths.

I must have slept but that was no dream.
The present woke beside me
sweating on the pillow
not worn out from all that running, only
breathless from the kick of it.

THE SHRINKING OF THE LENS

I used to open a door
and the square would dissolve behind me
the earth's embrace warm on my arms
trapezoids of sun dancing upon
my face beneath the grapevines
the smells of lime, *azáhar,*
wet earth after summer came in waves
the hustle of river and
air so fresh it bit my tongue.

Now the names have turned to hyperlinks
the square shrunk to a viewfinder
the landscape turned to crumbs
by thumbs so keen to share
they cannot hold their treasures
in a secret palm to love alone.

If I step back far enough
a Monet will emerge
of ads and amateur snaps
a figure springs out from the mess
reclining on a divan, elegant, serene.

She winks at me as she puts up
her feet on the Beast of Binary Code:
she is the Spirit of the Times, invisible
to faces glued to screens.

VETCH

Pulling vetch out of the thyme
velcro-fingered cleavers clinging
towering borage and bees for company
I rack my brain for that one word
in Spanish that holds this feeling
in its crook.

It isn't *satisfactorio,*
enriquecedor, or *realizador.*
I am, as they would say,
walking on the branches
dragging fingertips across
the cliffs and valleys of the bark
but never quite holding the trunk.

It came from a funny Sufi woman with
stained buck teeth who sold buttons;
she used the word once
when I gave her a ride
and it struck me but never
fully stuck. Unless
I made it up.

Pulling chickweed and
pallitory-on-the-wall
out of the land's most farflung lips
there is the orange-black striped slither
of *escalopendra* through the grass

each leg a scorpion's sting,
and there are
dozens of them.

I wait in the hammock for it to pass
and root around in the archives
worm-embroidered
lacy as dead leaves
in search of the match that
kindled this joy. It must
be a word for every
dirt-nailed dervish
hitch-hiking seeker
wild food forager
punctured by needles
from cardoons and nettles
hunting on still
ungloved.

Pulling pink-tipped white
earthsmoke out from
the charcoal of sodden earth
—to slice and douse in vinegar
and steep and strain and dose with—
this word buzzes round my head
bumbling about its business.
It is a word that predates
dictionaries; anyone
who digs enough will know
what it feels like

before the mouth
has had its way with it.

Orange blossoms. Nectar deep in
berryish buds burst
to pale trumpets: the smell
insists you close your eyes
the better to inhale it.

I can live without
knowing how
that word went.
The feeling is
enough.

THIS IS HOW YOU STROKE

Your touch is light:
most times I mistake it for
the itch of grass seeds inside sleeves
crunch of broken jam jar under shoe
piercing scream of dauntless daughter.

Your softness is so subtle I scowl. It
doesn't fit the silhouette of danger,
war, injustices that hurl me
into patient contemplation.

But disaster's only different
for my overlooking this caress
that turns to pinches,
swellings, lacerations
when it goes unrecognised.

This is how You stroke:
when there's no response,
no tingle of awakening, no purr
of pleasure or thanks, You strike.

I feel thumbnails
digging in, a Chinese burn
to the chest that would spell
a trip to the Headmaster's office
if You were a boy
but You are not.

These hands are wide-spread:
You offer candy or
the cane, and it would be cruelty
if you were a man
but You are not.

Your kindness is so vast
it offers room for ingratitude
gives us hands that throw down gifts
in a sulk and umpteen opportunities
to make amends.

Meanwhile
the handhold goes from friendly to firm
the tenderness turns terrible
and the stroke becomes restraint
before the precipice at our feet
—only then do we see
Your touch is always loving.

You prune us: we weep
to watch our aphid-ridden branches fall.

You shake us out: we wail
to see the dust desert us.

You scrub us: we fight
the pumice, clinging to dead skin.

This is how You touch:
smiling as we struggle

laughing as we swear
embracing even as we scratch and spit.

I wonder how we can be
worth the effort!

AROUND ME GREW A SECRET

On a bus stop bench today
opposite Crystal Palace park
a sphere of silver appeared
warped the passing buses
metal melted ads peeled off
bystanders blasted eyebrows singed
the trees flashed sauna-hot
and the curve of grey and drizzle lifted
I hid my laughter that
nobody seemed to notice while
the orb of clutter-thoughts
that dangle round my head
like strips of ripped skirt tied to branches
vanished. How they'd obscured the view!

Now it is clear those shabby tokens,
gifts given in hope of something else,
could never reach the Giver.
He does not do cupboard love, a
worship born of wanting—
"Take this time of mine but
give me what I wish for,
with all due respect. No, not that one—
I said I wanted it in red!"

But on the bus stop bench
around me grew a secret:
this is always here.

While we in earth robes walk
as though we're mountains
this is always here.

Once you've been shown it
you cannot unknow it.

This is always here.

TASBIH

It seemed a hiss
the drone of mating call
of insects lost in long grass
grating on short nerves
white noise on a muggy August eve
but that is just the speed
we think at, the pace
we expect all else to race to
and when their mindless buzz
is heard with their ears
it becomes
song
for no reason but to sing
because that is the thing that must
be done
in ecstasy at being small before the One

How many more songs are being sung
by entities so small and fast-lived
that their chorus doesn't register for us?

Too fine
cat's purr a thousand hertz wide
distant whirr of planetary slide
a jive when played apace with human lives
and now I hear sense in my daughter's cries
as tantrum slows to feverish high
I hear the words she tried to croon

the *Mama, listen, Mama, pick me up*—
a tune that spun on faster wheels
than mine, mismatching my headbeats
but that was the song her fever sang
the exultation expressed while my head was
too tight with longing for a quiet sleep
the silence of the stars as they creak past
or gentle buzz of crickets on a lawn
the white noise Nature gives the world-worn
so they'll find peace there
in music they can't hear

All things are in *tasbih*

for One Who is of all things

Aware

THE WHO OF YOU

My sadness is white paint
thrown onto walls from inside

The lack of you is making
backgrounds of me

Tensed in subjunctive mood
I've hung myself in frames, life

Hypothetical until
the *who* of you returns

Inks in my name and
calls my *who* back to its *from*

LOVE™

We regret to inform the public that
Love™ will no longer be available
in easy-to-swallow capsules,
with our patented time-release formula
and strict dosage developed to prevent
unhealthy dependencies.

Too many distasteful side effects
have unfortunately been reported
including:
dizziness   vertigo
loss of appetite
insomnia   rashes
bad teeth and
constipation.

Patients remarked that
after a short course they
were unable to manufacture love
for themselves, instead
relying upon our drug which,
though scientifically proven and
awarded dozens of accolades,
still left them feeling numb
and warmthless only minutes
after consumption.

It is a lamentable state of affairs
when a respected company (such as ours)

must remove from the market
such a rewarding product
leaving former users to find real love in its
notoriously haphazard
natural environment. Sufferers
may seek it out in fleeting conversations
with sweet-eyed strangers—a highly perilous act,
especially when they offer kindness—
or with their families (always dysfunctional),
their friends (clearly self-interested),
or simply
the unending life flow which
cannot be homogenized and therefore
one hundred percent
trustworthy.

We advise a steady course
of wealth collection,
building figures in your bank balance
and personae in your head
a comfortable home and
dependable career
and the accrual of esteem in
other people's reverent eyes
and let us not forget that one's worth
is built of countless tiny triumphs
one can rifle through like cash
when the Love™ thirst bites.
This will give a steadier appearance
of love in your lives, without any of
the inconveniences that actual love entails.

It is not, under any circumstances,
advisable to try giving your love
away, especially to people who
won't give any back. Remember—
love is like a cake: it's all about
how much you get to
eat yourself. The one who
baked it for you,
kind as they might be,
is nonetheless
irrelevant.

Please follow these instructions
to the letter, if you wish to survive
the tremendous withdrawal effects
of giving up your course of Love™.
There are as yet no studies into
the possible dangers of this ordeal.
It is a leap from the top of a
misty cliff, believing, dear clients,
you'll turn to birds and
fly away undaunted.
We take no responsibility
for your post-Love™ fates, and
we have the most
excellent lawyers.

THE JIHAD OF MOTHERS

The *jihad* of English people
is bearing the blankness of grey days
to wade through hourly petty gripes
without sinking into sourness

The *jihad* of postal workers is
going unnoticed except when they are absent
to remember how essential they are
even when never thanked

The *jihad* of mothers is trudging forwards
while a four-year-old pulls their hand backwards
to block out the screeching and the ingratitude
kicks, scratches and cusses and
still see a glow of hope around their kids

The *jihad* of café baristas in train stations
is to still feel life is new after making their
thousandth cappuccino

The *jihad* of company CEOs is
to tread water in crest and crash and
take the blame when blame is due
instead of laying off worker bees in swarms
while escaping in waxed Mercedes

The *jihad* of wives is to cycle through dozens of functions
—counseller, ironer, reminder of socks' destiny
in laundry baskets, confidante, financial adviser, alarm clock for
important events, shoulder masseuse, unwaged head chef

not to mention their *jihad* as mothers
and company CEOs or postal workers too—
while staying centred amid the spin

The *jihad* of husbands is to notice that cycle and
compliment them on it
and not be bewildered when their uncomplimented wives bawl

The *jihad* of doctors is to keep their hearts unglazed
even when administering their umpteenth death sentence
because the next they hear might be their own

The *jihad* of ease is to stay unmuffled
rejoin the whole instead of hiding behind alarmed gates
caressed by blandishments and easy fixes

The *jihad* of separation
is to bear the body's longing for closeness
without anaesthetising its need
or punishing it for its desire

It is all an uphill walk through muddy fields
with the four-year-old of your ego
tugging backwards on your hand
whining for ice-cream or a carry
a *jihad* that has no killer dimensions
only weariness
and loneliness
and fear that it is all in vain
waking each day as plain clothes warriors
each tiny struggle a chance to be
heroic

MOTHS

In the brittle night
moths converge
around a bold flame
pretender to the throne
while the sun's sovereign
rule is temporarily
out of town.

They flutter in an ecstasy
of scorching love, a
flittering impression
of shadow crowds
on the back walls
leaning in to hear the lines.

The wax is eaten steadily,
turned to smoke and puddles
while the flame burns taller
stretching up to compensate
for how it sinks.

And now with dawn
big brother swings around
slides over to the room
where little brother
has been entertaining guests
with tales of his illustrious
deeds.

How trifling, now,
its tiny blade of fire
beneath the thundering
brightness overhead;
how quickly all those powdery
achievements scatter, bruised
with light, eyes burnt, antennae
trembling.

        The shift in focus
was too brusque, the
disappointment lethal.
Tomorrow night there'll be
no wax left to smoke.

HERE

Every place I've ever prayed
—four wall frames for this
absorbing act of art
marking the spot where
the Beautiful appears
in hearts turned clear as
glass with love—
are visible again
if I conjure them
in *qiyam*: same *qibla*,
same calm.

The world aligns
these scattered squares
landscape provided by
the odd park, forest floor
or mountain slope
that ever served
as mosque
depth added by those
few times I prayed in *jama'*
one stroke of paint in *ruku'*, a
Van Gogh of backs and heads.

This is just the same place,
call it here or there.
Even though the compass
needle's moved

from Spain to India
Turkey, London
Washington, Marrakesh
my feet haven't changed;
my head still weighs the same.

So is there, in the same way that
there's only now, no past left and
no future yet to be,
no here, either?
No North or South
or East or West
no close to home
or far-flung nation
to judge one to be
God's homeland
visas rubber-stamped by
angels, everywhere else
a plane ride's reach
from the Real?

The scenery's been changed
but this stage has gone nowhere.
So many earths have crept
beneath my soles and yet
the solid rock beneath my brow
is deep as ever, its centre the same
the plunging in always the timeless
spaceless swim it ever was
wherever it has been.

With every *rak'ah*
the archived frames return
mirrored around
reflecting out
while I sit here
reflecting in.

BEING HOME TO SMALL BEINGS

Being home to small beings is like
        a stiff hike in the Himalayas
        elated and blistered
        the highs unworldly, views
        dizzying and you wake up in
        strange positions with a
        tent-mate's foot in your ear

It
        drains an inkwell in you, too
        leaves body parched for personality
        all vital juices trickled dry
        filling up again like milk ducts while you sleep
        pooling on sheets as you
        feed dreamt-of beings
        or a husband's leg grabbed in
        somnambulistic zeal

For this job you'll need
        glutes of reinforced steel
        biceps of titanium
        eight arms, rhinocerine skin and
        nipples of neoprene
        faces that don't mind
        being explored by curious fingers
        a contortionist's elastic frame and
        the stealth of a cat-burglar
        to slip away from sleeping babies

not to mention
a hypnotist's charm
a rugby referee's command
and a boddhisattva's ability to accept it all
smilingly

Equip yourselves, ladies!

This   is   no   mean   feat.

NIGHT BUS TO HACKNEY

Grime hangs in London's unlit streets
far from the gleam of white stone Aldwych
shy St Martin-in-the-Fields behind
a bridal veil embroidered with plane leaves
the dazzle of downward lines reflected on the Thames
from the blue, red, green South Bank
the baubles of the boats
and the owlish eyes of Big Ben.

I'm scrolling backwards now: I began in a
frantic fruitless race to meet my children's plane
on the worst night of the year. A torrent of
yellow Lycra would be cycling through town
tomorrow; trains were already disrupted now,
at midnight on a Sunday. Through the liquid flares of light
in my livid tears I hopped from Elephant & Castle
to Westminster (that travelcard bought
from the rosy-eyed skaghead at London Bridge
for 2 quid proved a godsend) and from there I walked
along Embankment, alone and children-less,
hunting down a Night Bus to Hackney.

(That day I'd been rugby-tackling 12 kids
into creative writing; the only thing
that seemed to grab them was the circular poem,
written on one face of a mobius strip.
A clever trick but it paused thoughts,
sentence cycling under the eye
like a pavement that keeps returning.)

Under the bridge the footpath was closed for works;
veering into the road a brilliant white coach slowed
as it passed me, just as the yellow LED
ticker tape read: ...to GODWARD ST.
I wanted to shout *Ya 'Aziz!* I call You and You answer!

Now my feet clicked on merrier, nose picking up old scents:
there was Savoy Street—I was where I understood.
Rounding Aldwych, a Scottish lass with gushing bloodied knee
staggered and laughed, a flurry of people
wide-eyed and foolish, shoelaces undone
with a sheen of vodka. I was safe
on a British belvedere among Russians
Bengalis and Koreans with maps.

I took the N26 towards Chingford and from the top deck
we passed Godliman Street.
For a city that scorns belief it is
Threadneedled into its fabric,
a Strand of awe stitched through its Petticoat:
a Bishop at one gate, a Moor at the other.

Once the protective shine of tourist attractions
gave way to Cambridge Heath and Columbia Rd,
despite its Decent International Store,
the gloom lurked in to leer at the lost.
Tattery fringes hung from mislit lamps;
a man wheeled an amp past, his friend
with blue ink smudged on his cheek wished me
a dreary *'Bo selecta'.*

All the while my company
was a Senegalese *dhikr*, of Allah and nothing else,
an ever-repeating refrain on mobius lips.

A HOLY SECRET SHARED

When they pulled us out
through the broken side window
the one I smashed with my cheek
as the car behind hit ours
—*oh my God oh my God oh my God*—
I saw a couple in their late 30s, perhaps,
soft, dark, kind eyes
but strong and wordless
familiar from I didn't know where
dark curly hair
she was shortish
soothing and solid as a nurse
who takes trauma in her arms daily
he was young, too, black-haired
colour in their cheeks
I turned to hug my seven year old
both sobbing with relief
pieces of blue shattered glass
on us, the seats, the edge
of the ditch we'd skidded into
metal violence of the impact
still shuddering in my bones
hot hurt on my face
blooming into a bruise
then our rescuers were gone
and a dozen others appeared
to console, assess damage to
the car—crushed concave

door lips now pressed eternally together—
help pledged
glasses of water fetched
the police in reassuring
yellow jackets appeared
from a restaurant down the road
embraces, explanations from the
man in the other car
his inflated airbags wilting and
cracked radiator weeping
"*This isn't what anyone wants, is it...*"
Later, the car towed,
we shored up at Casualty
the young doctor tearing his hair out
at the amount of paperwork to do
told me to touch my nose, his finger, here
here, there, and there
hammered my kneecaps
said I was lucky I didn't
break my cheekbone
—*luck!*—
The story spiralled
became a slip from death
in my recountings
as perhaps it was
packs of friends came by
like wise women bringing
organic praline and grape juice
to a giggling Mary with
half-Iranian baby Jesus on her lap
one even went home to bake us a cake

—luck!—
Five days later, I'd been
sick and sore, neck sprained
headachey but counting blessings
the baby wasn't in the back seat
where his car had caught ours
—luck!—
so musing I went to change a charger
at a computer shop where the couple
always seemed fed up of selling tech
disgruntled, pallid, he
prematurely white-haired, she
a towering bottle redhead with
glum green eyes and
lipstick disguising an unsmiling mouth
We haggled a bit: he complained
the keyboard I'd taken back worked fine
made me buy a better cable than
the one I'd planned to buy,
gave a wry laugh about the
capriciousness of wires
As I'm leaving he asks,
How are you after your crash?
I point to the faint emerald crescent
on my cheek, the tiny scratch fading.
Did you see the car?
We were there, he replies, in the car behind,
saw everything. Lucky he wasn't going so fast.
Lucky! They had to pull me out
of the window! I remonstrate.
That was us, he says quietly.

I pulled you out.
There is a glint
in his black irises
of a holy secret shared.
I struggle to pair this
slightly grumpy man
bored wife accomplice
with the couple in my memory:
It couldn't have been them!
Confused, I explain that
it all went blank,
thanked them anyway, backed out,
spinning. Did I repaint them,
in the panic of the moment,
hiatus in the reasoning mind?
Or was that a glimpse
of their best selves,
their waiting hero selves,
the strong, alive, kind selves
who are not worrying about returned keyboards
balancing books, the tedium of tablets
repeated conversations about
warranties and RAM?
That was not them;
that *was* them,
not disappeared, only
in waiting.

THE PEACE IT PIVOTS ON

I used to look for answers
in the warp and weft around
wondered what this fabric would be like
once every crease was ironed smooth.
The expanse of cloth was so endless it
hurt my eyes to keep looking
and all directions pulled me
'til I'd spun a skein of doubts
and arguments so thick their
soft accretion left me suffocated.

But every spool has a core
an empty space at its dead centre
where the dynamo that clothed it
finds the peace it needs to pivot on
the point of light in this vast swathe
that veils like night and we're
the pinpricks in it where the Infinite
broke through the cloth
so we could see.

Instead of looking for my needs out on
savannahs of plain cloth, I looked
into the emptiness within to catch
a heartful of that Light and then
the landscape fell quite smooth,
caught diamonds as they thundered
from the sky. Those are

the grains that form as Light contracts
upon our atmosphere, the mirrored discs
we sew upon our dress to make like
we're that night, here are our stars,
to spin our skirts and get tangled again
instead of staying still and owning nothing.

This is the night. We are its stars.

GLOSSARY OF FOREIGN TERMS
(Arabic except where otherwise indicated)

adhan: call to prayer

azáhar: (Spanish) orange blossom

batata harra: spicy potatoes (a Middle Eastern dish)

bombona: (Spanish) butane bottle used for cooking and heating

cantaora: (Spanish) female flamenco singer

dunya: material world

escalopendra: (Spanish) scolopendra, a poisonous centipede

'ilm: Islamic sciences, religious knowledge

'isha: night prayer

dhikr: remembrance of God; a gathering in which *dhikr* is recited or sung

'Eid: Islamic festival

falafel: chickpea and lentil croquettes

fana': extinction (in God)

fatha: Arabic vowel sign, 'a', written as a stroke above the letter

hadra: presence; Sufi breathing practice used in dhikr

Hayy: Alive; one of the 99 Names of God

khubs: bread

miswak: Salvadora persica twig, traditionally used for cleaning teeth

'oud: agar wood incense

qibla: direction of Mecca

qiyam: standing upright, one of the positions of the Muslim ritual prayer

ra: letter of the Arabic alphabet

rak'ah: unit of ritual prayer consisting of standing, bowing and prostrating

realizador: (Spanish) fulfilling

ruku': bowing, one of the positions of the Muslim ritual prayer

Sami Allahu man hamidan "Allah hears the one who praises Him", phrase said during the ritual prayer

satisfactorio: (Spanish) satisfying

shikamoo: (Swahili) respectful greeting, lit. "I touch your feet"

Surat al-Ikhlas: In the Qur'an, Chapter of Sincerity

tasbih: glorification of God

thali: (Hindi) selection of vegetarian dishes

Ummah: international community of Muslims

wudu': ablutions before ritual prayer

za: letter of the Arabic alphabet

INDEX

ABOUT THE AUTHOR

Medina Tenour Whiteman was born in Granada, Spain, in 1982
to English-American Muslim parents, and was raised in the UK.
She holds a BA (hons) from SOAS in African Language
and Culture and is the co-author of
A Travel Guide to Muslim Spain (Huma Press).
She lives in Spain with her husband and three children.
Her website is www.cavemum.com.

www.ingramcontent.com/pod-product-compliance
Lightning Source LLC
Chambersburg PA
CBHW020913090426
42736CB00008B/608